A SHORE THING

Poems for Ocean Explorers

T.M. Ramsay   M. Pepiciello

To Curious Kids Everywhere,

The more you know, the more you'll grow.

T.M.R

Copyright © 2024 by T.M. Ramsay

Illustrations by Martina Pepiciello

ISBN 978-0-9953446-2-4 (Hardcover)
ISBN 978-0-9953446-1-7 (Paperback)
ISBN 978-0-9953446-3-1 (E-Book)

All rights reserved.

No part of this publication may be used, reproduced or stored in a retrieval system, or transmitted in any form or any manner - electronic, mechanical, recording, or otherwise - without written permission from the author, except in the case of brief quotations embodied in critical articles and reviews.

Library and Archives Canada Cataloguing-in-Publication Data available.

A SHORE THING: Marine-themed educational poetry for children; No age specified.

Contents

- 4   Catch Of The Day
- 5   Interview With A Star
- 6   The (Not-So) Common Octopus
- 8   Rocky Beach Balancing Act
- 10   Periwinkle Paths
- 11   Mighty Blue Mussels
- 12   A Marine Mystery
- 14   Hermit Crab, Hermie
- 16   Sand Dollar Anchors
- 17   Flotsam And Jetsam
- 18   My Atlantic Lobster Tale
- 20   Ode To Jellyfish
- 22   Beach Goers
- 23   Greedy Green Crabs
- 24   Sand Dollar Test
- 26   Green Sea Urchin
- 28   Beach Day
- 30   I See Seashells
- 31   Glossary

Catch Of The Day

Herring gull stood on sandy beach,
Waiting for some tasty treats
To wash around his pink webbed feet.

Waves he watched with yellow eyes,
Hoping for a sweet surprise –
A crab, a snail, or fish with fries.

Bird bent his head with yellow bill,
Tossed seaweed that formed a hill,
Finding only empty shells.

He turned about and spied a S'more,
Three green grapes, one apple core –
Thought herring gull, *What a score!*

With one *Long Call* – a seven-part shriek,
This compost collector of the beach,
Gulped the grub then soared to sea.

Interview With A Star

Starfish or Sea Star - which name do you like more?
I have no scales, fins or gills, so Sea Star I prefer.

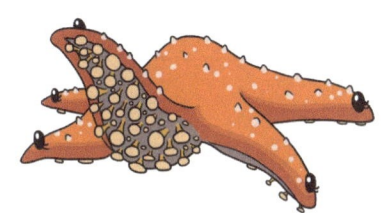

Sea Star, tell me how you move and how far can you go?
With many tube feet, I slowly crawl one mile per week or so (1.6 km).

Can you tell me why you have an eye on each arm tip?
My simple eyes sense light and dark, so guide me on my trips.

What will happen to you if you lose one of your arms?
I'll grow it back, but not like that, in a year – no harm.

I know that you are carnivore, so what prey do you hunt?
I love bivalves inside hinged-door shells, but the shells I do not munch.

With your very tiny mouth, how can you eat prey larger?
My stomach comes out through my mouth and melts prey down to chowder.

Sea Star, you are one cool beast. I enjoyed our talk today.
I did too, now hunger calls, so time to slurp away. Good-day.

The (Not-So) Common Octopus

Alone and along the dark ocean floor,
I slink, saunter, crawl and wander –
Fishing for shellfish snacks.

Sucking in water and squeezing it out
Zooms my body all about –
Roaming the briny blue.

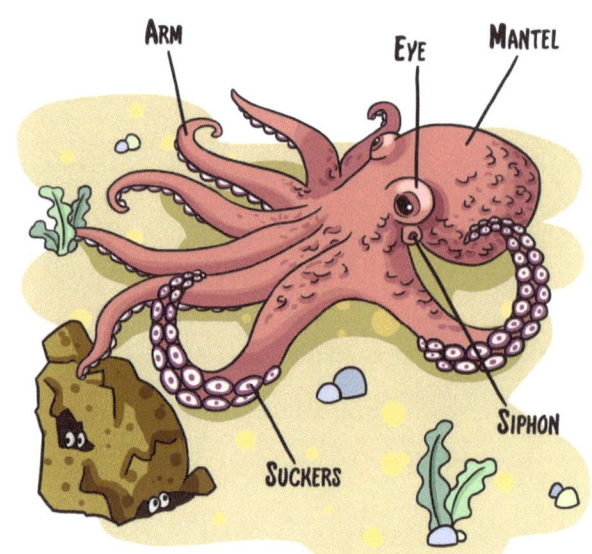

Eight sucker-lined arms – pull, swing and sway,
Work on their own in an organized way –
Probing, smelling, tasting, coiling, clinging.

In dark or light, I see with ease.
I spy a fisher's trap and squeeze
My bendy bod through trap-door hole,
Nab a crab then *Whoosh* – I go.

I tend to flee from looming danger –
First, shoot ink to confuse invader,
Then time to make my hasty escape
Using jet propulsion and torpedo shape.

Whales, sharks, dolphins – I try to avoid,
Big slimy eels make me cringe and hide
Beneath a rock or in a crevice.
Camouflage I also use to mask me from my menace.

Alien-looking creature, Chameleon of the Sea,
Brilliant escape artist, Brainiac – all me.
I love problem solving. I am Super Cephalopod!
Yet, I'm called a COMMON Octopus –

Don't you think that's rather odd?

Rocky Beach Balancing Act

I study the wonky beach rocks
As my eyes trace a perilous path.
Deep breath, then…
Ca-Carefully, I step.

Stones sharply shifting,
I lean with all toes gripping,
Return to solid footing…
Ca-Carefully, I step.

I'm teetering then tottering,
Arms wavering, legs wobbling,
Which way rock tips is just a guess…
Ca-Carefully, I step.

Sizzling sun is burning me,
Blinding rays – can hardly see,
This slimy spot – so slippery…
Ca-Carefully, I step.

Whipping winds attacking hair,
Forced to gulp harsh salty air,
Must keep going – almost there…
Ca-Carefully, I step.

Crisscrossing rocky beach terrain
On ground that plays such shifty games,
With nature's forces joining in
Is NEVER easy…

In my flip-flops.

Periwinkle Paths

Plentiful periwinkles,
On rocks in tidal zones,
Moving at a snail's pace,
Up – over – down.

Mucous glue sticks winkles to
Slick rock walls as they climb.
Flat fleshy foot is the part
That pulsates each along.

As they creep, little sawtooth tongues
Scrape algae from the rocks.
It's an all-you-can-eat buffet feast
For these tiny gastropods.

Mighty Blue Mussels

Around sea docks, clinging to rocks,
Sat clusters of dark bluish shells.
I tugged to take one – a strange sensation,
Like hauling hair from a brush.

A fisher strolled by and chimed,
"Y'know why mussels are glued in clumps?
Each has a foot gland that makes thin sticky strands –
Strong fibres called byssal threads.

"These elastic strings cling to rocks and hard things –
Then waves can't bash mussels about.
They're safety ropes too, in tidal pools,
When sea gulls pop in to pluck out."

He went on his way, and I, right away,
Gazed on those glossy blue shells,
Then stooped again for close inspection
Of these marvellous marine animals.

A Marine Mystery

On rocky salty shorelines,
In shallows you may spot,
Cream-coloured cones
Firmly fixed to rocks.

What are these bundled funnels –
Each sliced across the top,
These hard sharp domes
With a piggy bank slot?

Are they mini volcanoes
That are in deep sleep?
Sun-bleached magic mountains –
A trap door at the peak?

Maybe alien birdies –
Bitty beaks poking from nests,
Or mystical marine teepees
Protected by jagged edges.

Perhaps they're cyclops eyeballs –
Big bulging eyes half-closed,
Or enchanted pixie dresses
That twirled about then froze.

Now if a slot slides open,
And a feathery fan appears,
These mini mounds are none of these
For this mystery has cleared.

Each cone is an animal –
A creature quick to elude,
For the fan are legs of a barnacle
And it's waving those legs to trap food.

Hermit Crab, Hermie

Hermie lives beneath the waves –
Always on his own.
A snail shell is the preferred place
He likes to make his home.

Hermie crab is growing fast,
So shell is feeling tight.
He knows well it's time to move –
The house hunt starts tonight.

Out shopping for a fitting shell
Is one tough task indeed,
For he will lug his house until
He finds just what he needs.

Not just any shell will do –
The size must be just right.
Then he can safely tuck inside –
Away from all that bite.

Hermie spots an empty shell
And parks along the side.
He quickly crawls from old to new –
To try it on for size.

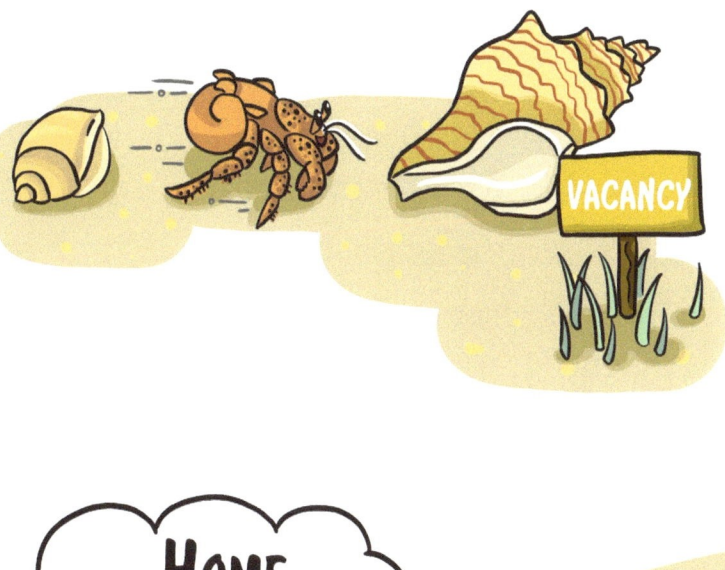

Shell's not too big, not too small,
Nice shape – a spiral cone.
So Hermie stays to settle in
His new hand-me-down home.

Sand Dollar Anchors

Sand dollar animal – small, round and light,
Has many a method to keep it from flight,
Depending on ocean's movement and might.

When calm waters nudge the soft ocean bed,
Sand dollar stands on rounded edge,
Slightly buried in the sand
With tightly packed spines anchored in.

When rough waters stir the sandy sea floor,
Sand dollar grips its ground much more
By lying flat like a Welcome mat
Or tilling down into the ground.

When churning seawaters become a torrent,
Sand dollar battles the strong undercurrent
By gulping big grains of sand to add weight,
For heavier body can anchor in place.

Flotsam And Jetsam

Jetsam met Flotsam while drifting at sea.
Cried Jetsam to Flotsam, "I'm in misery.
Storm hit, bashed my ship, to-and-fro it rolled.
Then the crew, in a flash, cast me overboard!
So here I float, no port in sight, stranded all alone.
My fleeting friends are gulls and fish –
 I never will see home."

Then Flotsam said, "You were tossed to help lighten the load.
You saved your craft and crew. Don't fret about an abode.
My story is a sadder one," said Flotsam as he bobbed.
"An accident cursed my ship – all aboard were lost.
It all sunk, I stayed afloat, and I will tell you now,
Better to be riding waves than a thousand fathoms down!"

My Atlantic Lobster Tale

My head boasts four antennae,
I rock a long segmented tail,
Five pairs of legs, two beady eyes
That see movement, but not detail.

I use eight skinny legs for walking –
Tiptoe on limbs like sticks.
Still, I can flee, swimming backwardly,
With speedy strong tail flicks.

My two large claws look different,
For each one has its work:
Big claw to crush, small claw to rip –
They are a lobster's knife and fork.

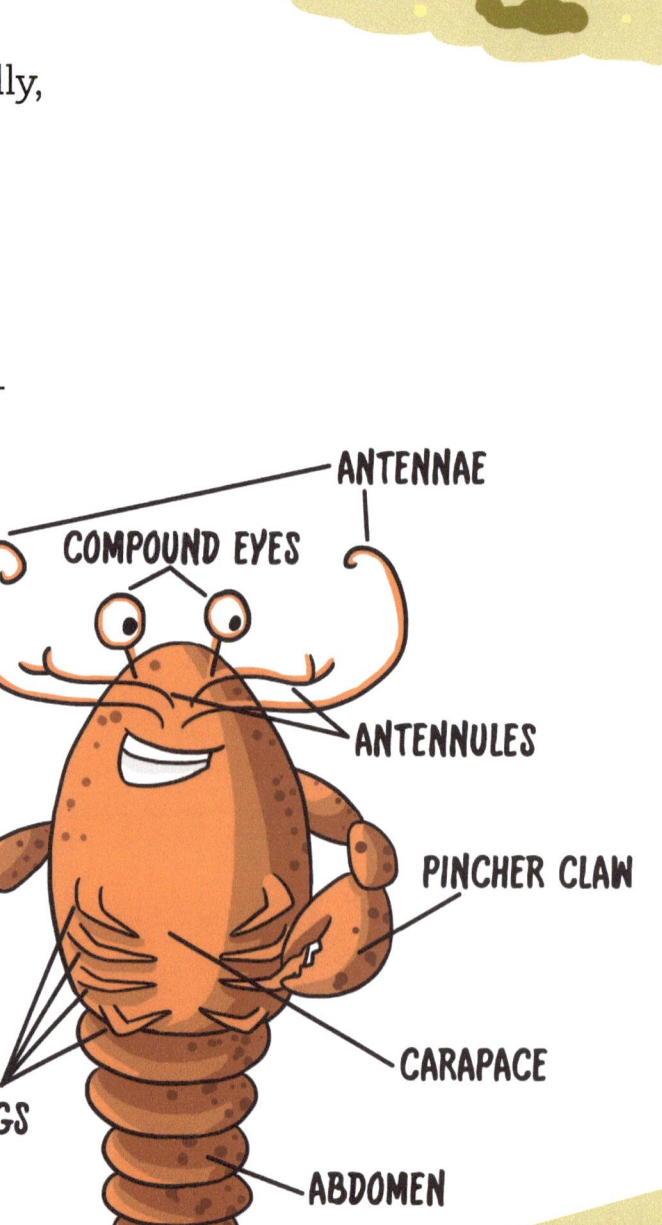

My shell is an exoskeleton
That I must shed to grow:
Twenty-five times in my first six years –
That's a lot of moulting, I know!

When I shed my shell, I'm in danger,
For my body armour is gone.
So I hide until I form a new hard shell,
Which may take six weeks or beyond.

I live under rocks and in crannies,
Hang out on the ocean floor,
Eat molluscs, fish, plants and I scavenge.
This makes me an omnivore.

Ode To Jellyfish

Oh, Jellyfish – they are not true fish,
For a backbone they don't have.
Gummy globs without heart, blood, brain –
To some this sounds quite sad.

But I know there is more to view –
Not just boneless brainless beings,
For jellies have cracking qualities –
I'll explain just what I mean.

Jellies are great survivors,
Found in oceans over the world,
Been thriving on earth millions of years –
Showing up before the dinosaurs.

Some are luminescent,
For they make and give off light.
This attracts prey and keeps predators at bay,
Then they won't swim in and bite.

Jellies are not fast swimmers,
And often choose to ride the currents.
But how they know which way to flow
Is a mystery in science.

Their flowing frilly arms
Funnel food up to their mouth.
Whatever jelly's gut cannot digest,
Jelly's mouth will poop back out.

Jellyfish range in size –
From teeny to bigger than a man.
With stinging cells on dangling tentacles –
Please avoid them if you can.

Beach Goers

Strolling the beach on a hot summer's day,
You'll spot many fine folks on full display:
Silent sun worshippers soaking up rays,
Snorkeling swimmers exploring the waves,
Balancing boarders spilling with splashes,
Cuddling couples in rose-coloured glasses,
Gold diggers swinging metal detectors,
Hawk-eyed parents watching their youngsters,
Sandcastle builders with majestic plans,
And one talking head poking up from the sand.

Greedy Green Crabs

Bully bodies on the hunt,
Destroying eel grass while looking for lunch.

Clams, oysters, mussels, fish?
Grab Whatever is their favourite dish.

Always hungry – Never full,
These alien invaders keep marching still.

How to stop them? No one can say.
It seems greedy green crabs are here to stay.

Sand Dollar Test

If combing the beach and you spy,
Cast upon the land,
A pale-coloured coin-like shell
With petal pattern, so grand,
You discovered a sand dollar case –
The endoskeleton – a final trace.

When sand dollar was alive,
Living on sea floor,
It looked quite different from this hollow disc –
It was so much more,
With many types of body parts,
Working together, from bottom to top.

The shell, called a *Test*, used to be dressed
In short velvety spines.
These bendable quills could trap and trek
And burrow beneath the brine.

The petal design, etched on the top,
Was five paired rows of pores.
From these holes, tube feet poked out
To help with breathing chores.

The mouth was on the flat underside –
At the centre hole.
The star-like shape was hair-lined grooves
And paths for foods to flow.

Now you know a little more of the striking
Sand dollar test.
But before you go, I make to you
One important request.

If combing the beach and you spy,
Stranded on the land,
A purplish prickled coin-like shell
Hiding petal pattern, so grand,
Gently toss it back to sea –
This is where living dollars should be.

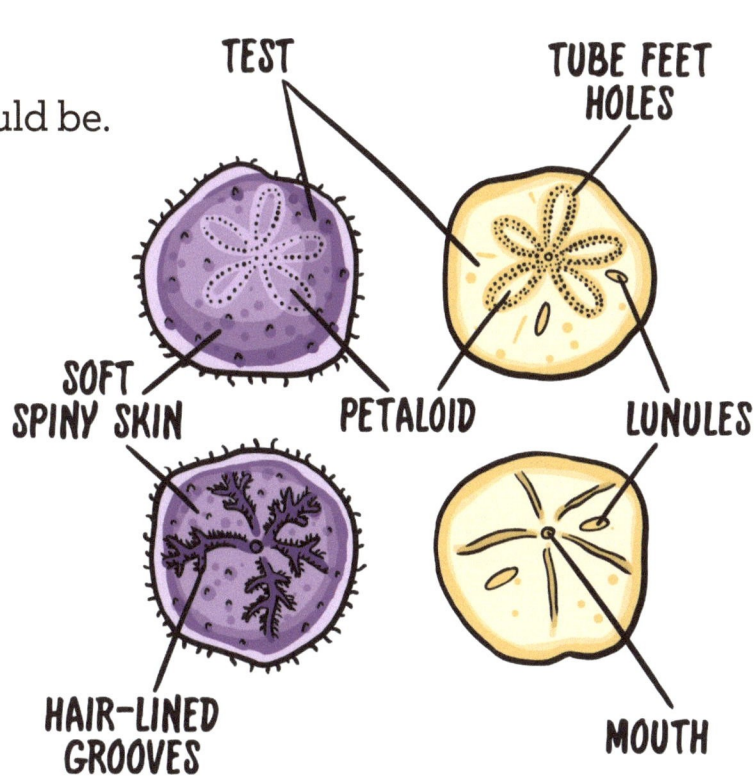

Green Sea Urchin

Spiky Sea Urchin,
You are Hedgehog of the Ocean
With your dome-shaped body of spines.
Each prickle you can point
In the direction that you want –
For each sits in a ball-and-socket joint.

Roaming Sea Urchin,
Rows of tube feet keep you movin'
With their built-in suction cup tips.
You suck in water through top hole,
And out your feet it flows –
Creating force to pull you to-and-fro.

Strange Sea Urchin,
Your mouth is *Aristotle's Lantern*,
Named for a famous Greek thinker.
Inside a plated jaw,
There are five sharp teeth that gnaw –
Scraping algae from rocks like a claw.

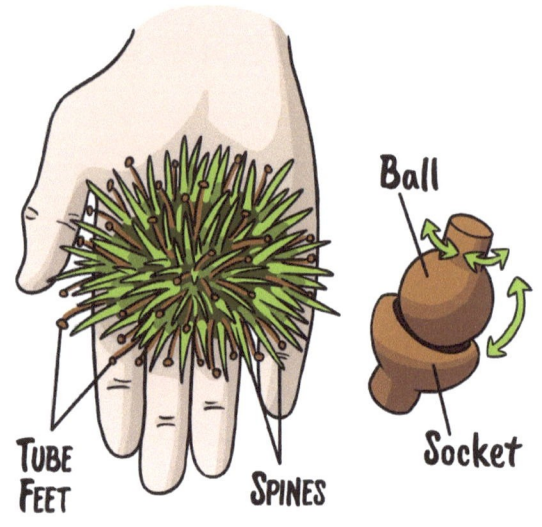

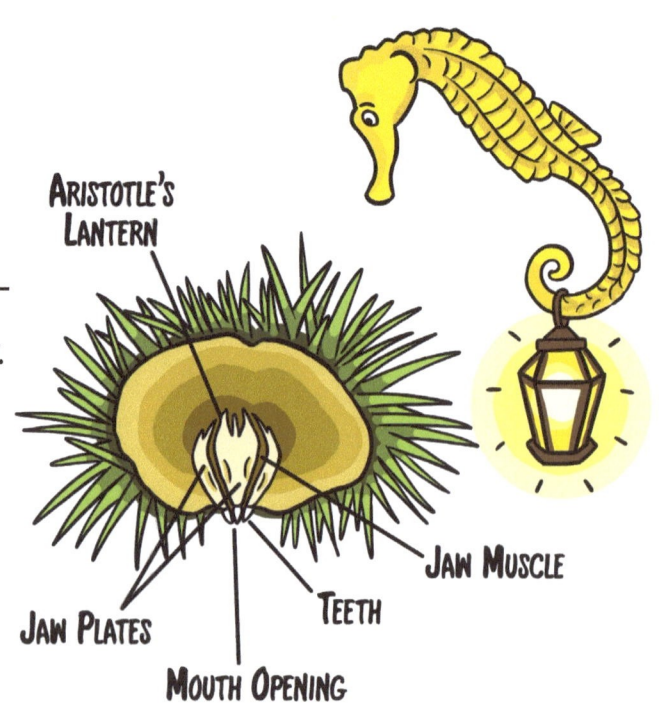

Hungry Sea Urchin,
You are always out searchin'
For your all-time favorite fare.
On kelp you love to bite,
And other seaweed types –
Chomping down plants, day and night.

Wary Sea Urchin,
Predators are likely lurkin',
Hunting for you amongst the kelp.
Crabs and sea stars, too,
Are keen to dine on you –
Stiffen up your spines to make them *Shoo*!

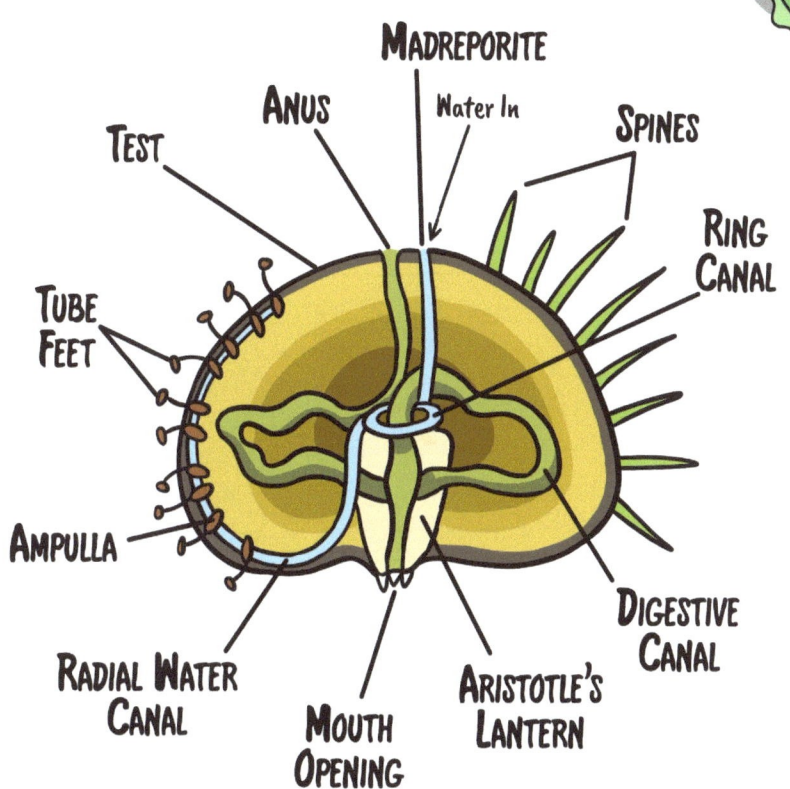

Beach Day

Parking car,
Popping trunk,
Load up arms,
Close trunk, CLUNK.

Swashing waves,
Balmy breeze,
Seagrass sways,
Feeling free.

Groups galore,
Stop and scan,
Spy a spot,
Lead the clan.

Spread out blanket,
Unfold chairs,
Slather sunscreen,
"Jump in!" dares.

Waves slap ankles,
Slowly wade,
In-and-out,
Must be brave.

Shouts and squeals,
Strokes and jumps,
Buckets and castles,
Time to munch.

Open cooler,
Treats in tums,
Back to waves,
Splish-Splash fun.

Growing shadows,
Cooling breeze,
Shake and fold,
Find car keys.

Flip-flops on,
Planks to walk,
Heading home,
Quiet talk.

I See Seashells

Pointy, Rounded, Oval, Long
Sanded, Banded, Brittle, Strong
Ribbed, Coiled, Pearly Whorls
Spiky, Spiraled, Chalky Swirls
Faded, Raided, Cracked, Chipped
Speckled, Freckled, Animal Nipped
Fat, Thick, Wafer-Thin
Creatures Out, Creatures In
Lumpy, Bumpy, Silky Smooth
Silty, Gritty, Grimy, Grooved
Domed, Coned, Flat, Cupped
Scalloped, Hinged, Open, Shut
Bleached, Beached, Caked, Slimed
Bowled and Holed, Over Time
Dull, Polished, Heavy, Light –
My favourite shells are Glossy White.

Glossary

Algae Marine plants that do not flower and have no true roots or leaves

Bivalve Marine soft-bodied animal with a hinged double shell - (E.g., mussel, clam, scallop)

Brine Seawater, very salty water

Byssal Threads Silky strings made by the foot gland of a blue mussel

Cephalopod Marine boneless soft-bodied animal, suckered tentacles, well-developed head/eyes

Current Body of water moving in a certain direction

Endoskeleton Inside skeleton of an animal

Exoskeleton Outside skeleton of an animal

Fathom Unit that measures water depth - (1 fathom = 1.8 metres or 6 feet)

Flotsam Floating debris from a shipwreck or shipping accident - (Compare with Jetsam)

Gastropod Soft-bodied animal usually with a shell and living in water - (E.g., snail, lobster)

Jetsam Floating debris thrown overboard to try and save a ship - (Compare with Flotsam)

Kelp Large brown seaweed with a long tough stem

Luminescent Glowing

Marine Found in or produced by the sea

Mollusc Soft-bodied animal with no backbone and usually lives in water - (E.g., snail, octopus)

Moulting Shedding shell (or skin) to allow for growth

Mucous Slime secreted by animals for protection and easy movement

Omnivore Animal that eats both plants and animals

Predator Animal that hunts other animals for food

Prey Animal that is hunted for food

Segmented Divided into parts

Tentacles Thin flexible limbs, feelers

Tidal Pools Shallow puddles of seawater on rocky intertidal shores

Tidal Zone Area that has daily tide action (E.g., a beach)

Torrent Powerful fast-moving stream of water

Tube Feet Body part made up of small bendable tubes with suction cup tips

Whorls Spirals, curls, coils

Common Octopus

Atlantic Lobster

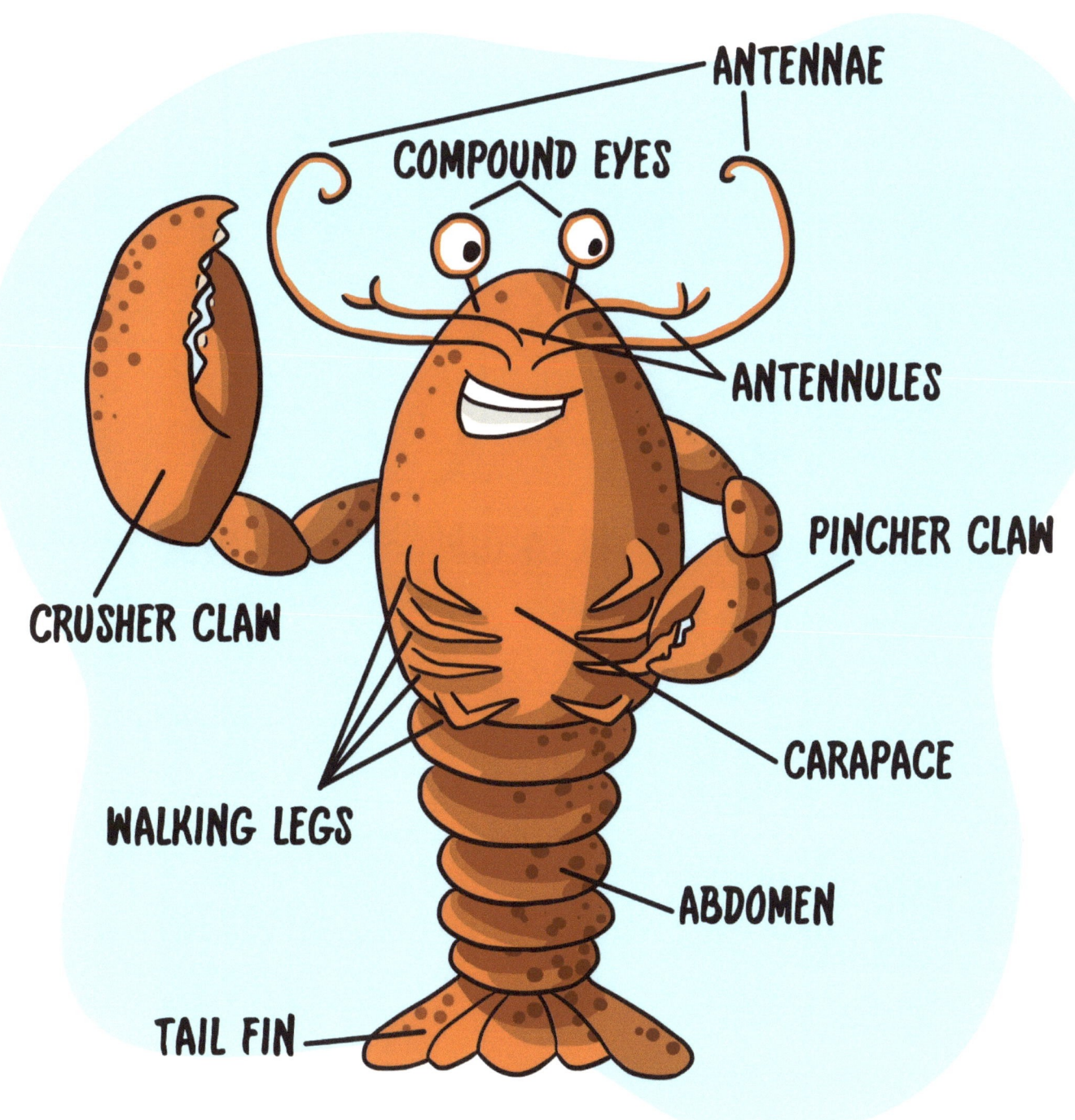

33

Sand Dollar

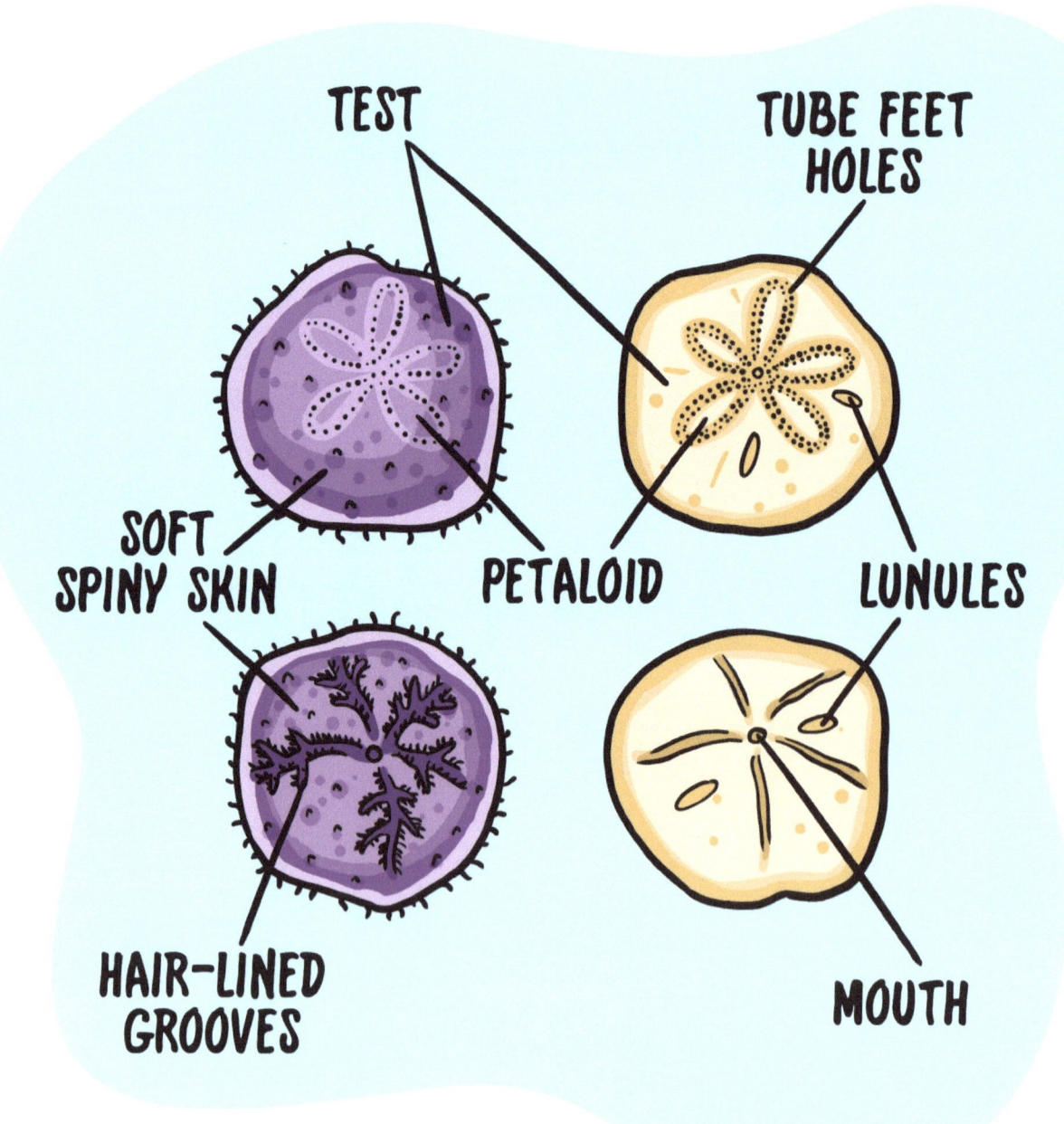

Green Sea Urchin

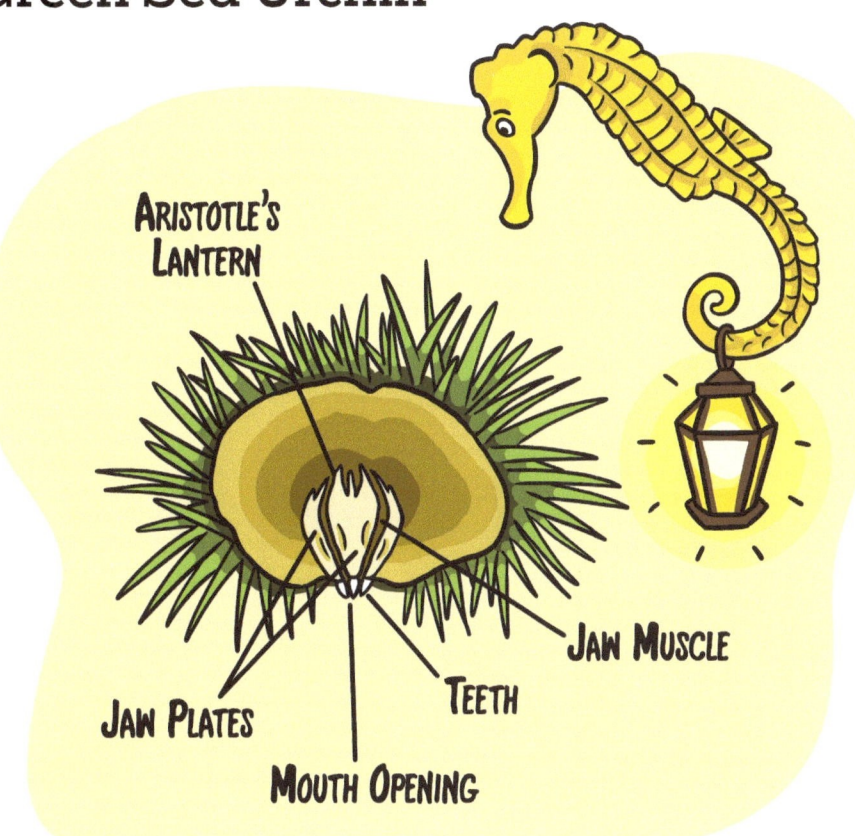

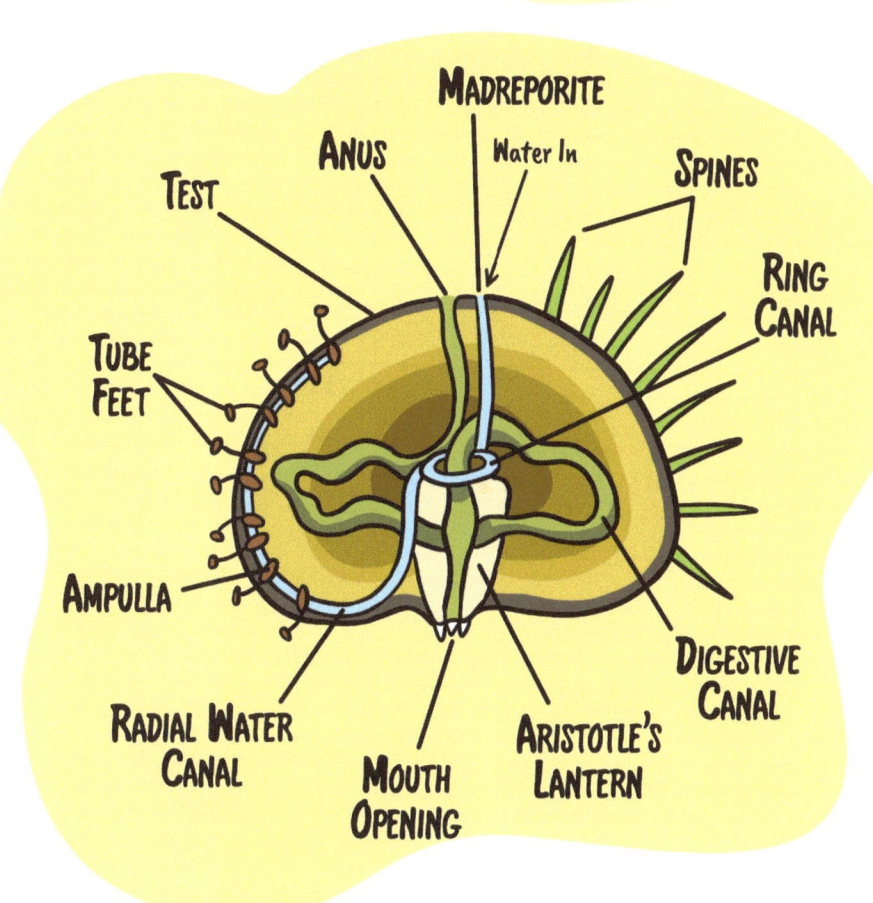

MARINE JOKES

- Why are fish so smart? → Because they live in schools
- Why did the crab cross the road? → To get to the other tide
- Where does an octopus like to sleep? → On a seabed
- Why are oceans so strong? → They have a lot of mussels
- Why don't scallops like to share? → Because they are shell-fish
- Where do whales get their teeth fixed? → At the orca-dontist
- What time do sharks visit the dentist? → At tooth-hurty
- How do jellyfish make clams laugh? → With ten tickles (tentacles)
- Where do you weigh a whale? → At a whale-way station
- How do fish talk to each other? → They use speech bubbles
- Why don't skeletons go scuba diving? → They don't have any guts
- What is a shark's favourite game? → Swallow the Leader
- What do sea monsters like to eat? → Fish and Ships
- How do snails call their friends? → On their shell phones
- What kind of hair do oceans have? → Wavy

A SHORE THING – Poems for Ocean Explorers is a collection of fun marine-themed educational poems written in rhythm and rhyme. It was specifically designed to help kids develop language and literacy skills while encouraging curiosity and caring for the ocean and its creatures. Why rhythm and rhyme?

- **Enjoyable & Engaging:** Builds positive association with books and reading
- **Sound patterns:** Lays the foundation for phonics and early reading success
- **Pattern Recognition & Prediction:** Develops logic and sequencing skills
- **Memory & Language Development:** Strengthens recall, literacy, vocabulary
- **Self-Esteem & Confidence:** Strengthens conversational and social skills
- **Environmental Awareness:** Expands knowledge base and increases caring

About the Author

T.M. Ramsay grew up near the ocean, is a snorkeler, scuba diver, sailor and beachcomber. She spent years teaching English and sharing the magic of language with students of all ages. Now, she combines a passion for teaching with a passion for the water, creating playful, rhythmic poems that invite children to share in her wonderful discoveries and to make their own discoveries too!

www.ingramcontent.com/pod-product-compliance
Lightning Source LLC
Chambersburg PA
CBHW041430090426
42744CB00002B/26